# POP GEMS OF THE 1960s

## CONTENTS

— PIANO LEVEL —
EARLY INTERMEDIATE/INTERMEDIATE
(HLSPL LEVEL 4-5)

ISBN 978-1-4234-2564-9

7777 W. BLUEMOUND RD. P.O. BOX 13819 MILWAUKEE, WI 53213

Visit Hal Leonard Online at
**www.halleonard.com**

Visit Phillip at
**www.phillipkeveren.com**

# AND I LOVE HER

Words and Music by JOHN LENNON
and PAUL McCARTNEY
Arranged by Phillip Keveren

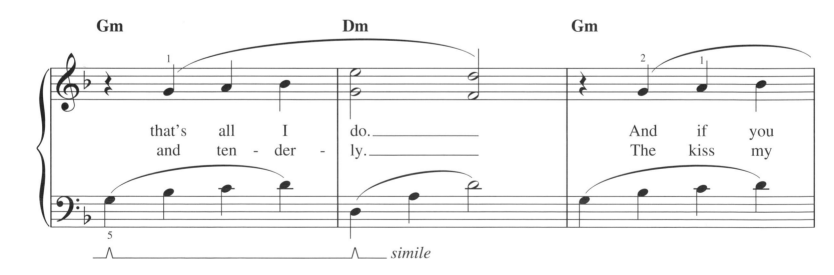

**Gm**  **Dm**

Bright are the stars that shine,

*mp*

**Gm**  **Dm**  **Gm**

dark is the sky. I know this

**Dm**  **B♭**  **C**

love of mine will nev - er die, and I

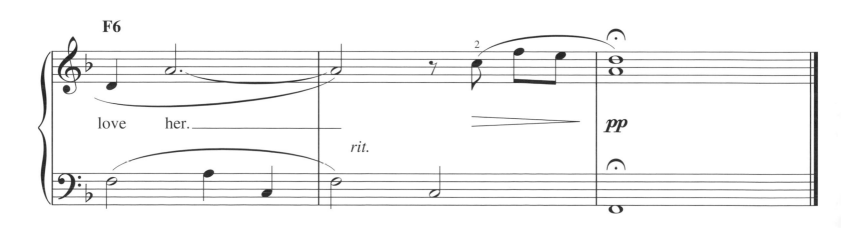

**F6**

love her.

*rit.*

*pp*

# BLUE VELVET

Words and Music by BERNIE WAYNE
and LEE MORRIS
Arranged by Phillip Keveren

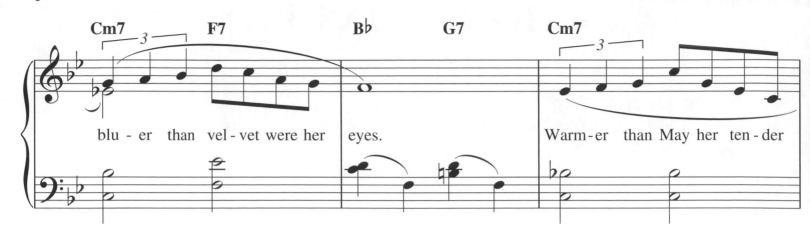

blu - er than vel - vet were her eyes. Warm - er than May her ten - der

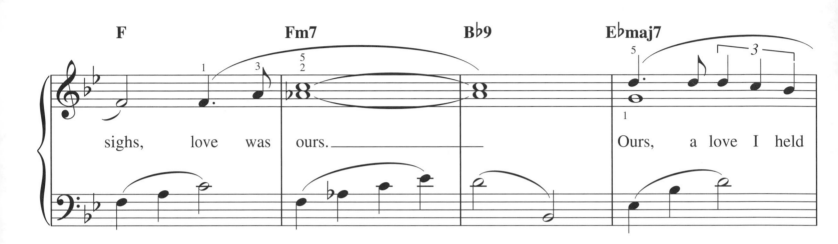

sighs, love was ours. \_\_\_\_ Ours, a love I held

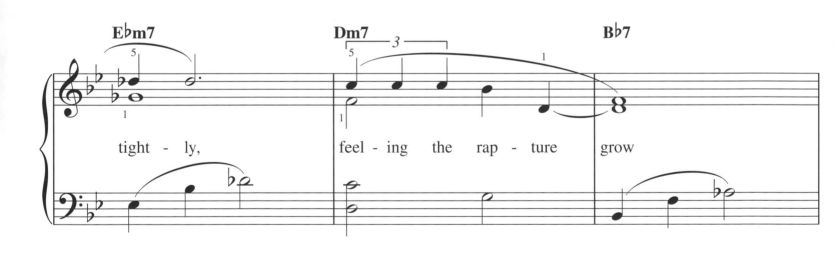

tight - ly, feel - ing the rap - ture grow

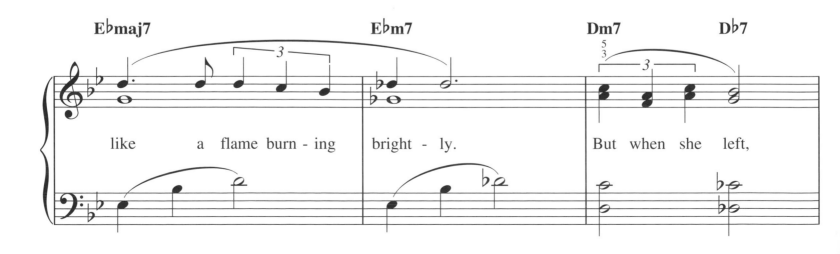

like a flame burn - ing bright - ly. But when she left,

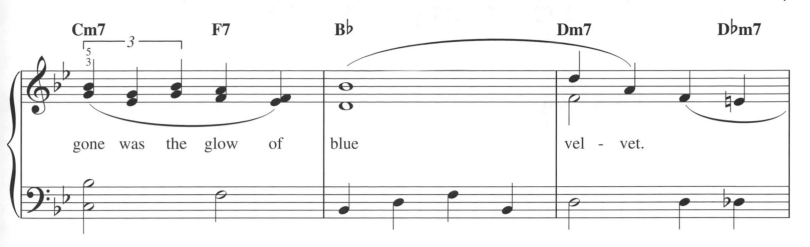

gone was the glow of blue vel - vet.

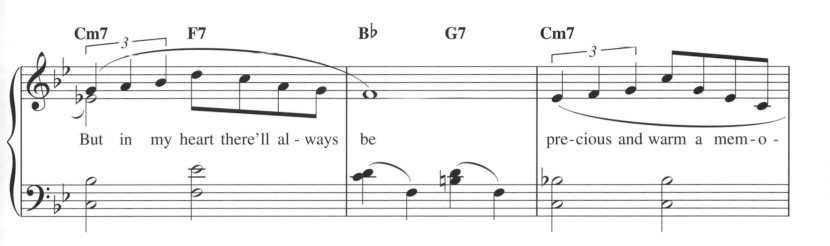

But in my heart there'll al - ways be pre-cious and warm a mem-o -

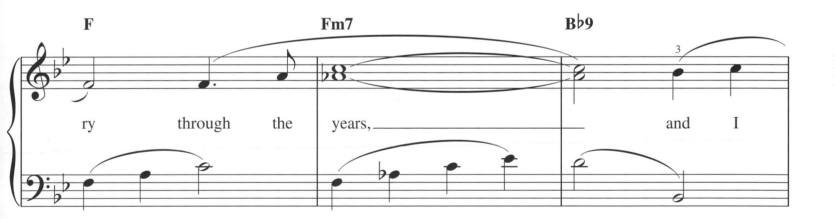

ry through the years, and I

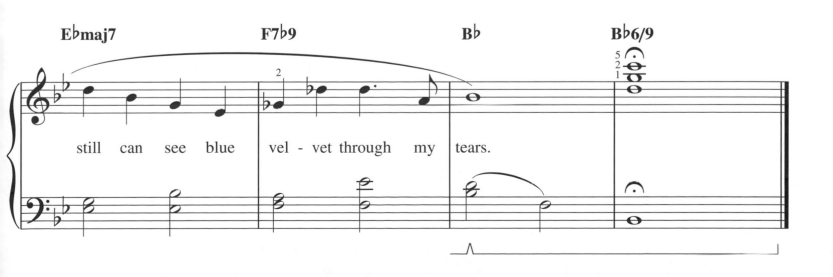

still can see blue vel - vet through my tears.

# BEYOND THE SEA

By ALBERT LASRY and CHARLES TRENET
English Lyrics by JACK LAWRENCE
Arranged by Phillip Keveren

# CAN'T HELP FALLING IN LOVE

from the Paramount Picture BLUE HAWAII

Words and Music by GEORGE DAVID WEISS,
HUGO PERETTI and LUIGI CREATORE
Arranged by Phillip Keveren

With tenderness (♩ = 76)

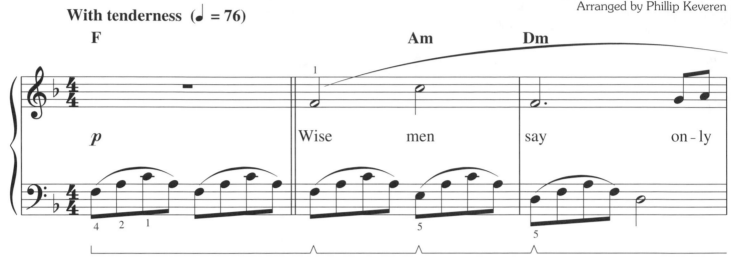

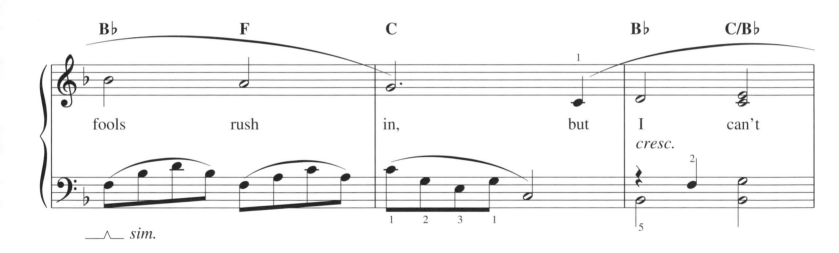

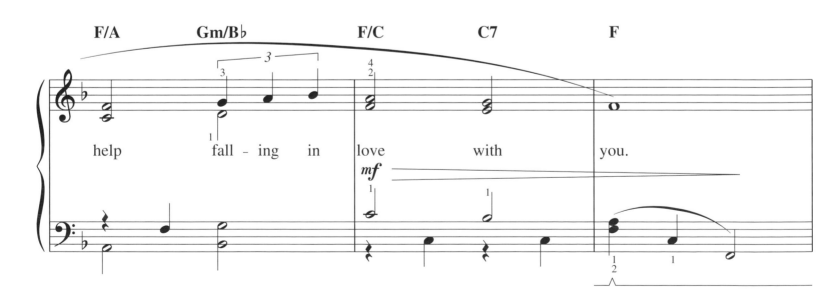

# CHERISH

Words and Music by
TERRY KIRKMAN
Arranged by Phillip Keveren

how man-y times I've wished that I had told you, you don't know
not gon-na be the one to share your dreams,— that I am

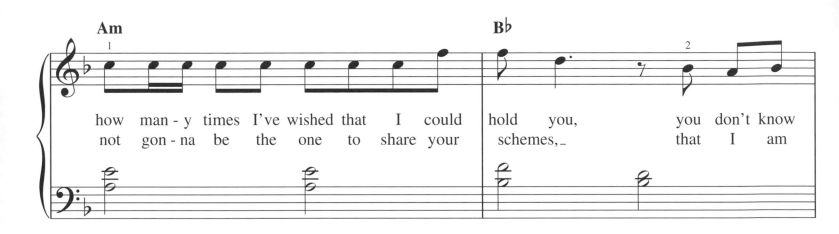

how man-y times I've wished that I could hold you, you don't know
not gon-na be the one to share your schemes,— that I am

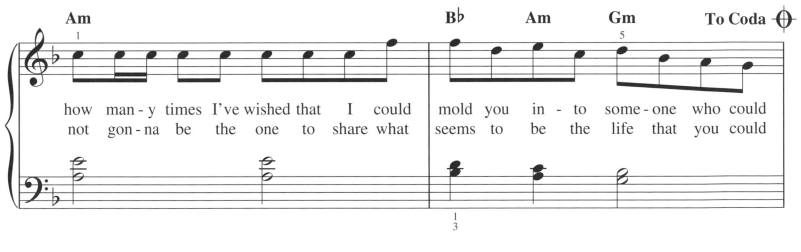

how man-y times I've wished that I could mold you in-to some-one who could
not gon-na be the one to share what seems to be the life that you could

cher-ish me as much as I cher-ish you.—
cher-ish— as much as I do—

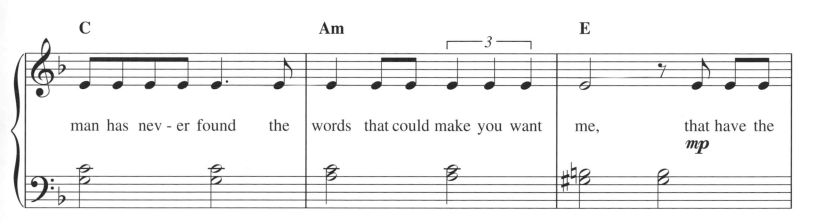

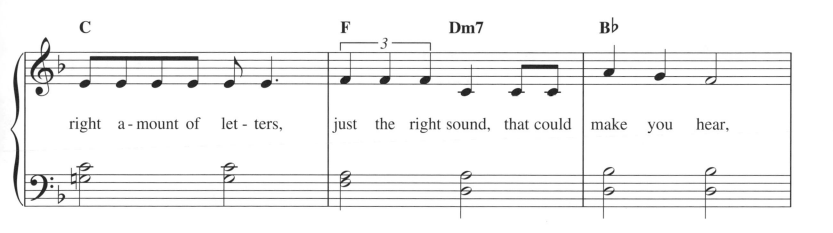

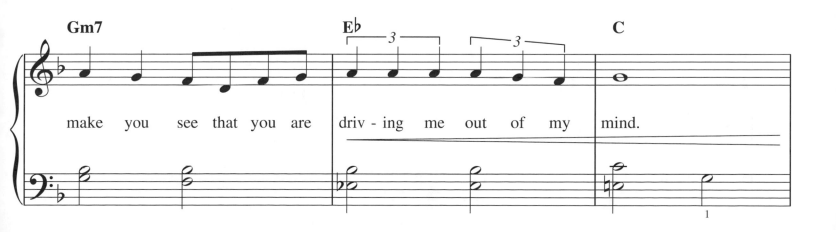

18

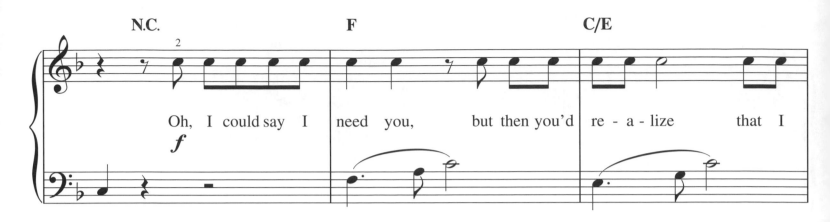

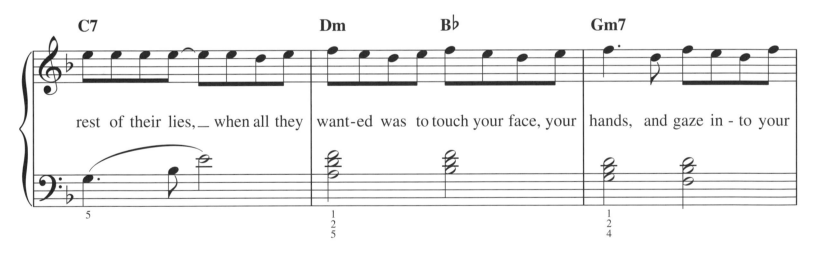

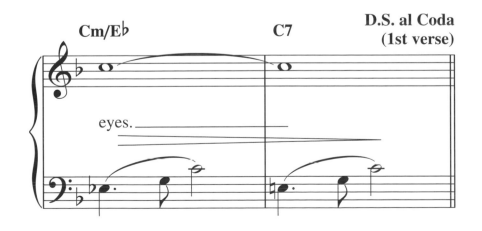

19

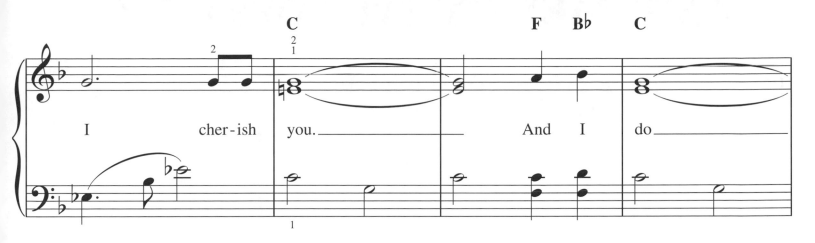

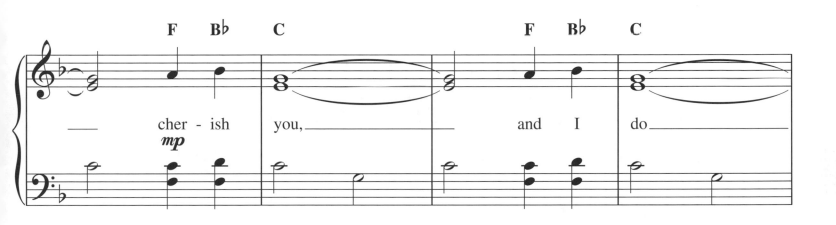

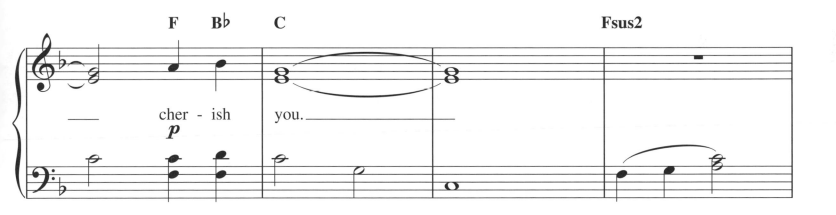

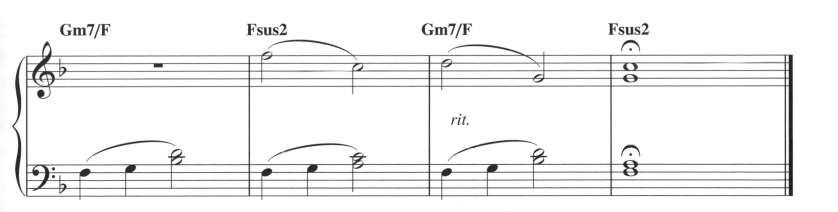

# CAN'T TAKE MY EYES OFF OF YOU

Words and Music by BOB CREWE
and BOB GAUDIO
Arranged by Phillip Keveren

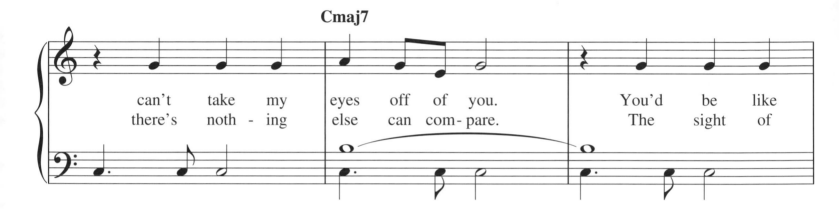

God I'm a - live.
know that it's real.

You're just too good to be true,

can't take my eyes off of you.

Par - don the
*mf*

22

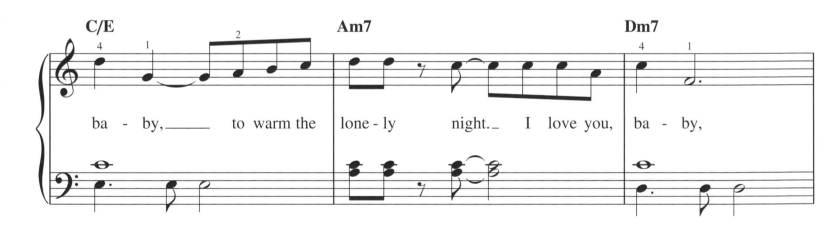

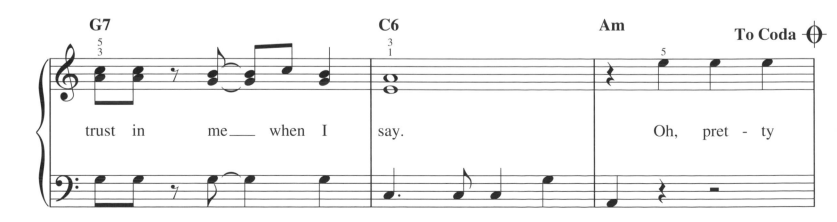

ba - by,_____ don't bring me | down, I pray._ Oh, pret - ty | ba - by,_____ now that I've

found you, stay,_ and let me | love you,_ ba - by. Let me

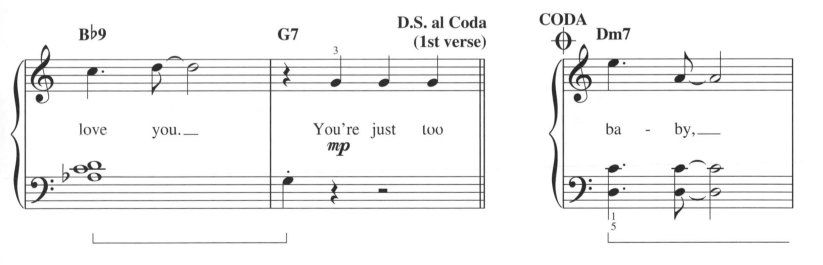

love you._ | You're just too | ba - by,_

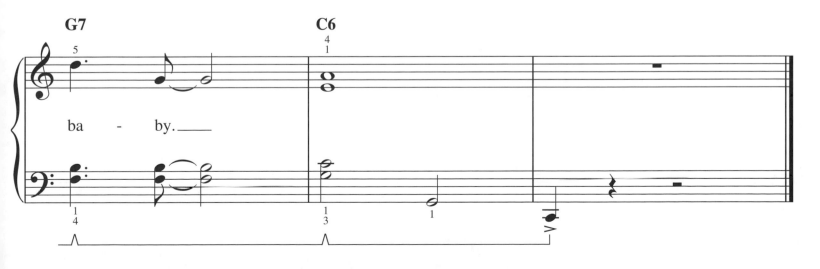

ba - by._____ | |

# EVERYBODY LOVES SOMEBODY

Words by IRVING TAYLOR
Music by KEN LANE
Arranged by Phillip Keveren

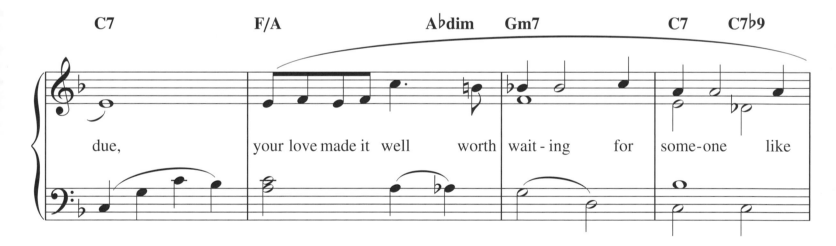

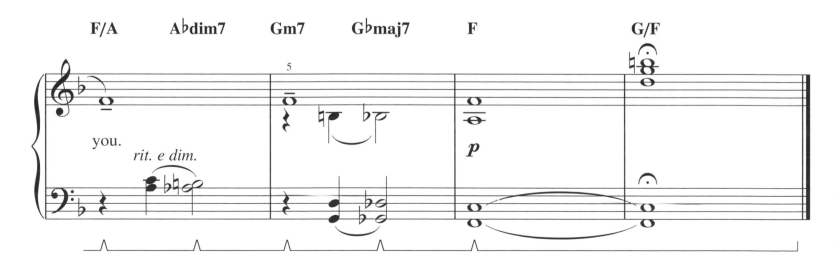

# STRANGERS IN THE NIGHT
## adapted from A MAN COULD GET KILLED

Words by CHARLES SINGLETON and EDDIE SNYDER
Music by BERT KAEMPFERT
Arranged by Phillip Keveren

28

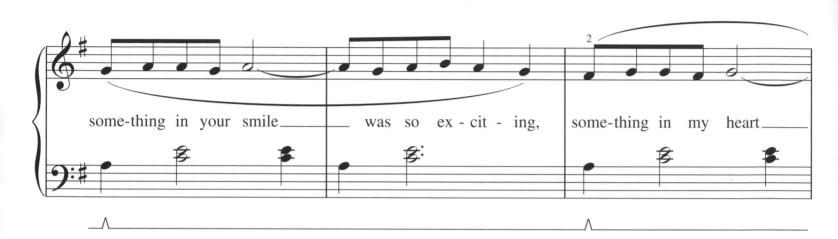

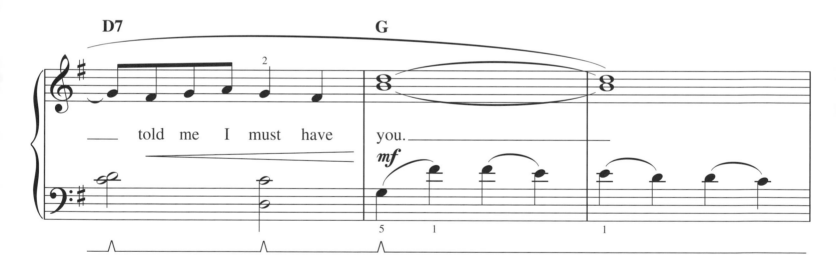

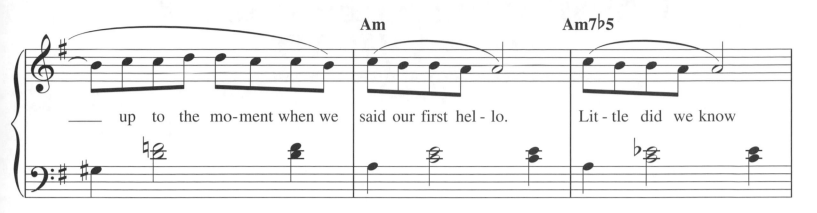

_____ up to the mo-ment when we said our first hel-lo. Lit-tle did we know

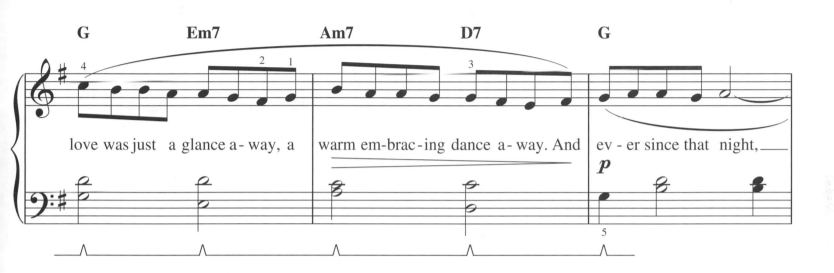

love was just a glance a-way, a warm em-brac-ing dance a-way. And ev-er since that night,_____

_____ we've been to-geth-er, lov-ers at first sight,_____ in love for-ev-er.

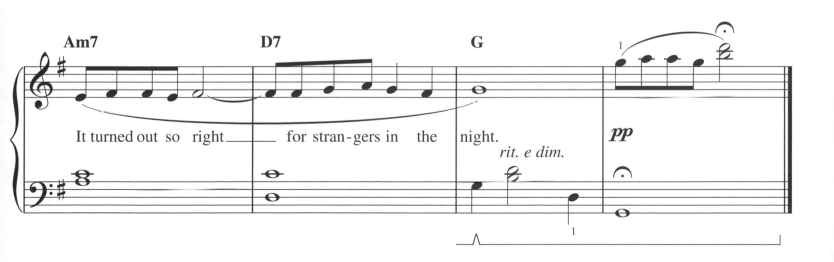

It turned out so right_____ for stran-gers in the night. *rit. e dim.*

# RAINDROPS KEEP FALLIN' ON MY HEAD

### from BUTCH CASSIDY AND THE SUNDANCE KID

Lyric by HAL DAVID
Music by BURT BACHARACH
Arranged by Phillip Keveren

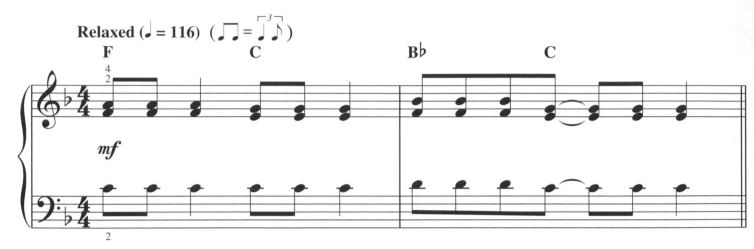

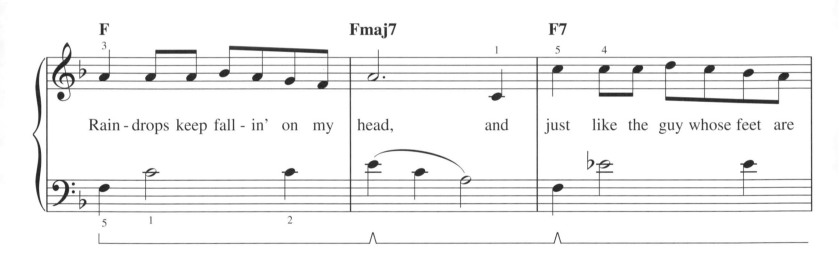

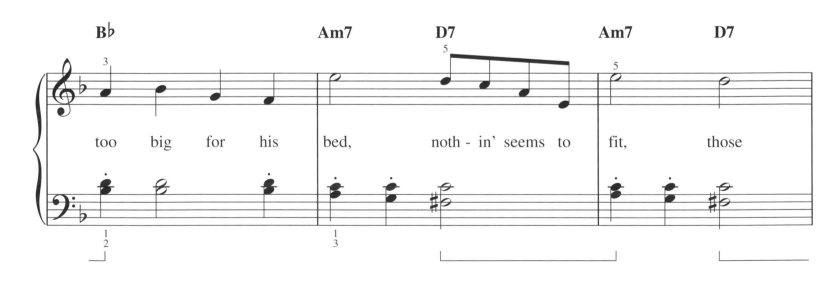

31

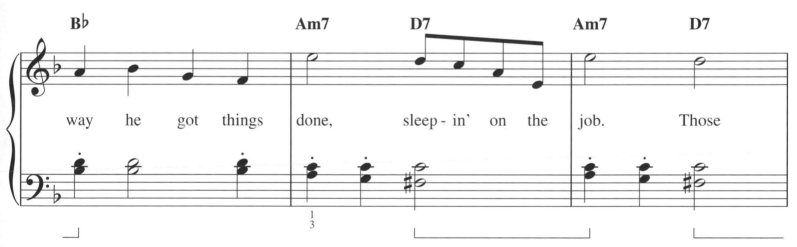

# SUGAR, SUGAR

Words and Music by ANDY KIM
and JEFF BARRY
Arranged by Phillip Keveren

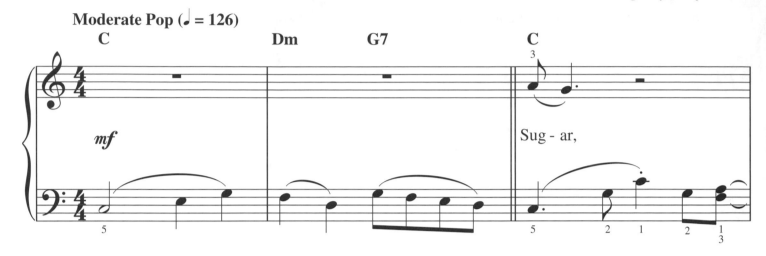

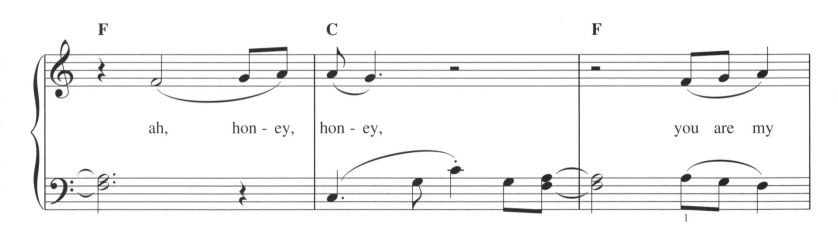

# THERE'S A KIND OF HUSH
## (All Over the World)

Words and Music by LES REED
and GEOFF STEPHENS
Arranged by Phillip Keveren

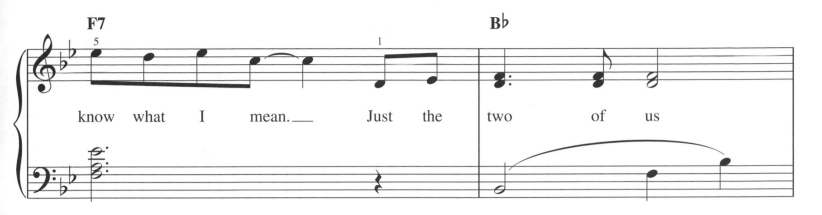

know what I mean.___ Just the two of us

and no-bod-y else___ in sight,___ there's no-bod-y else___

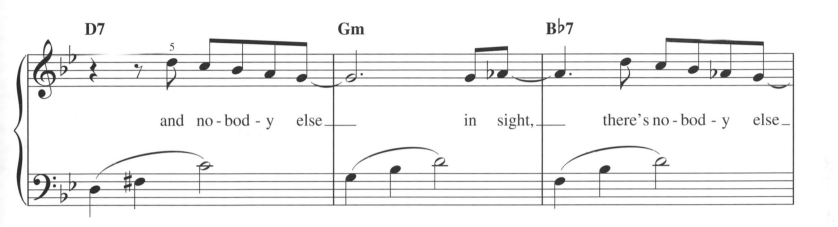

___ and I'm feel-ing good___ just hold-ing you tight.

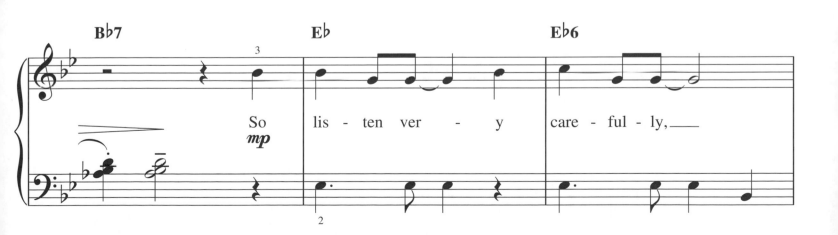

So lis-ten ver — y care-ful-ly,___

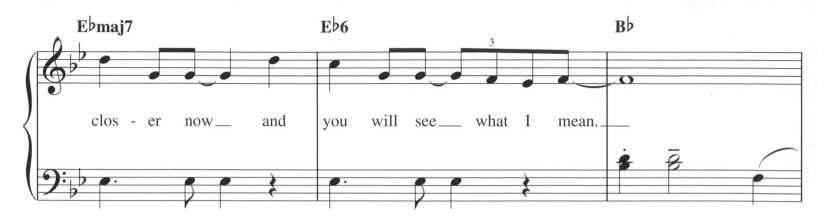

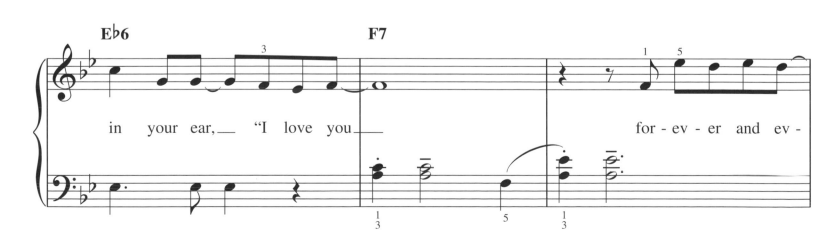

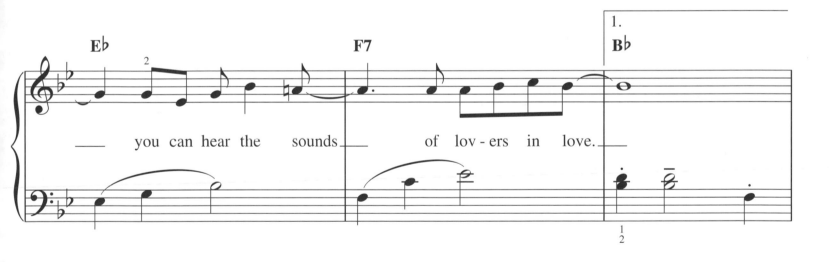

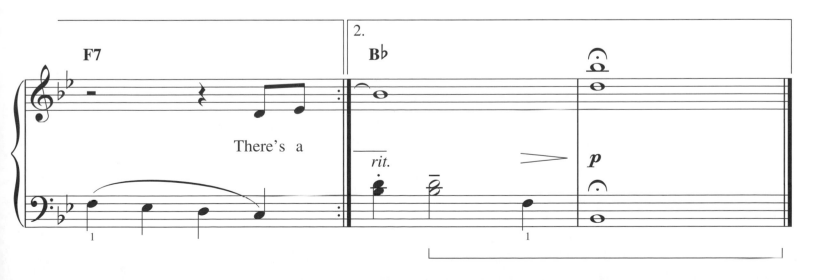

# THIS GUY'S IN LOVE WITH YOU

Lyric by HAL DAVID
Music by BURT BACHARACH
Arranged by Phillip Keveren

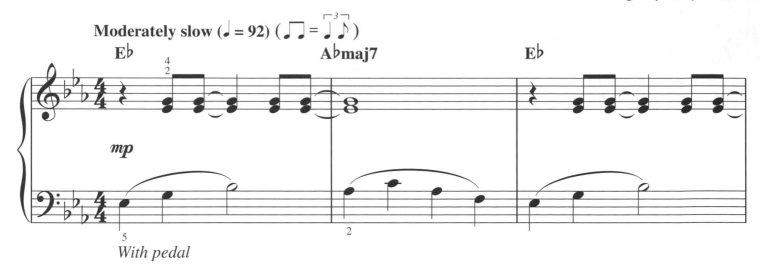

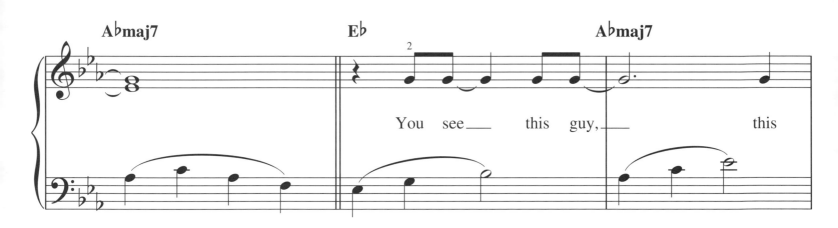

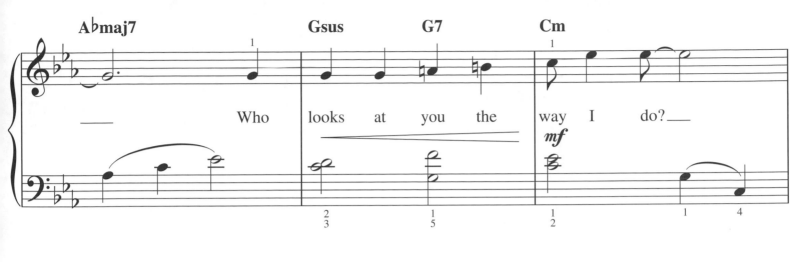

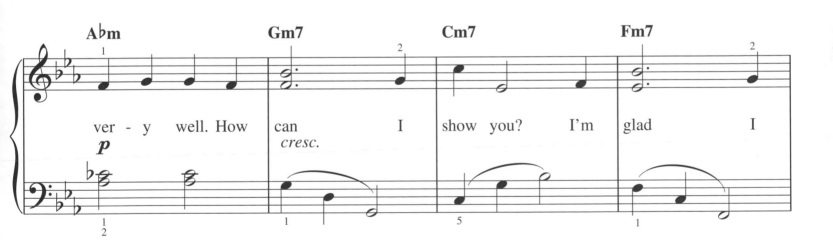

44

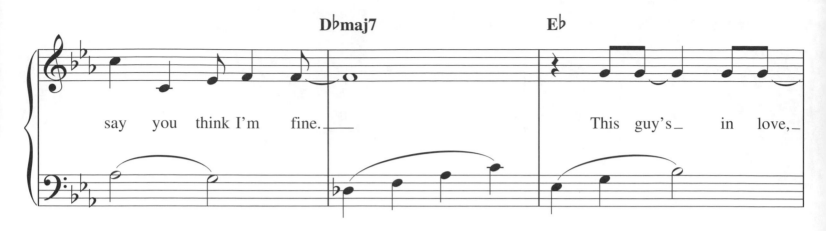

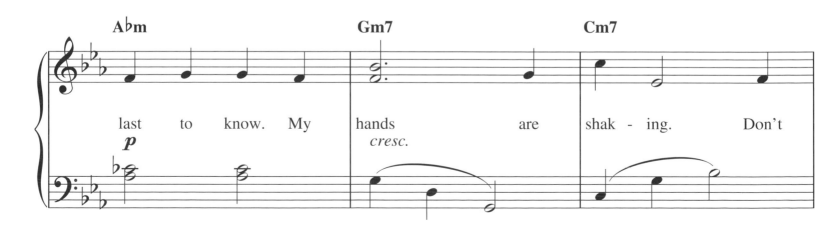

# WINDY

Words and Music by
RUTHANN FRIEDMAN
Arranged by Phillip Keveren

**Moderate Rock** (♩ = 138)

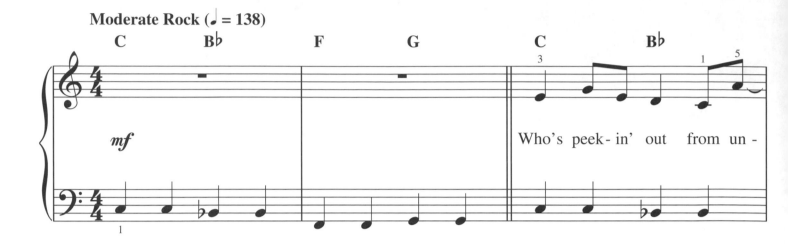

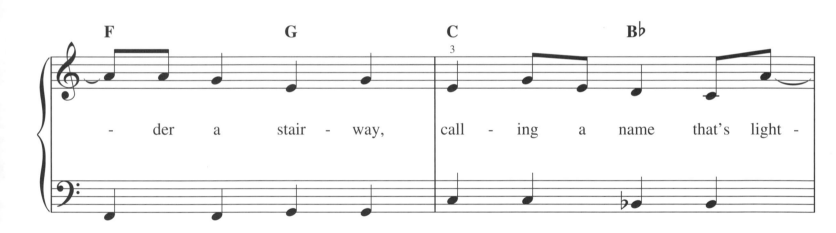

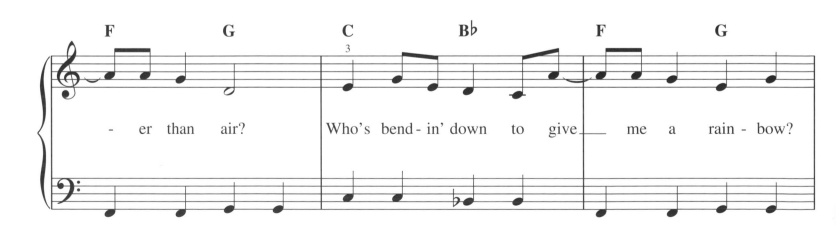

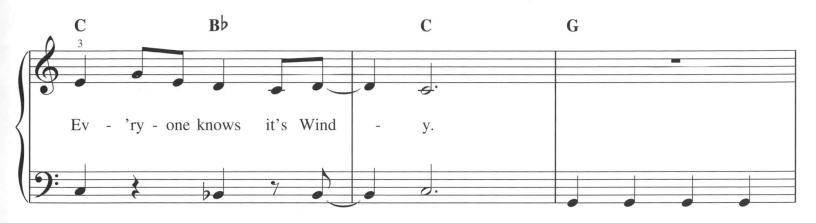

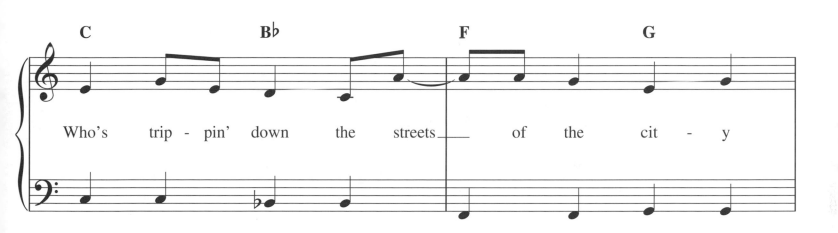

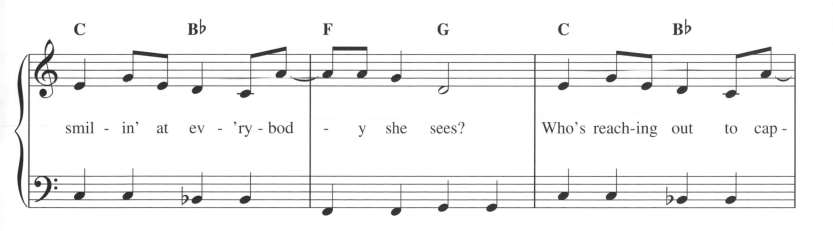

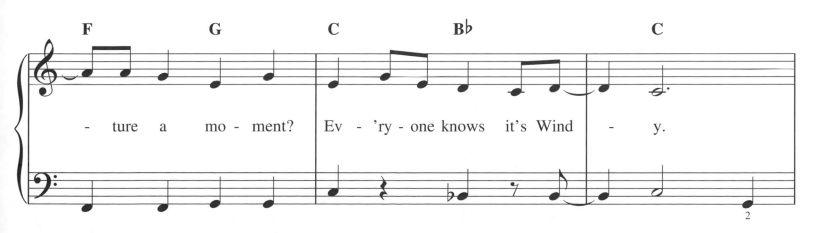

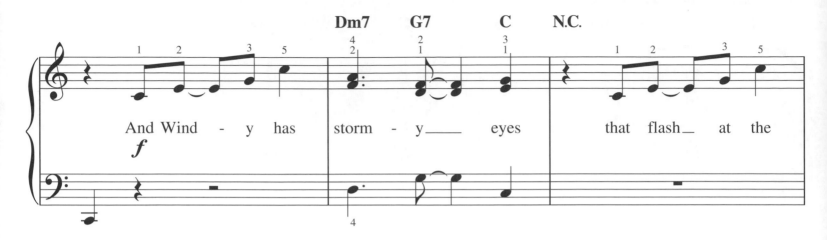

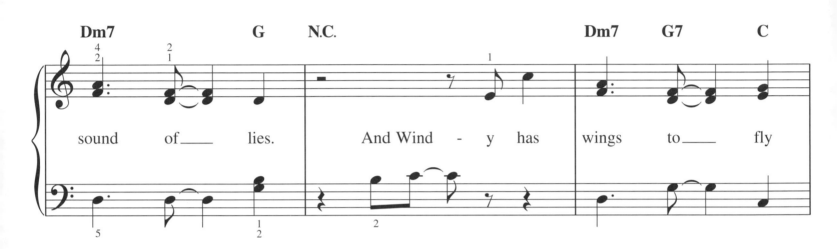

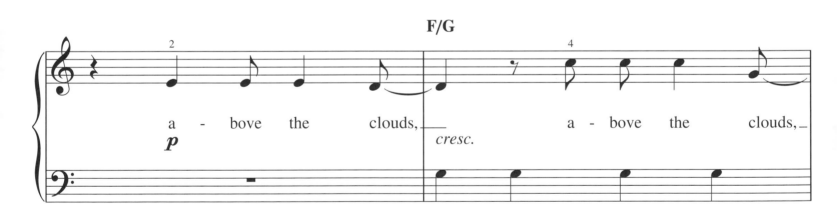

Who's peek-in' out from un - der a stair - way, call - ing a name that's light-

*mf*

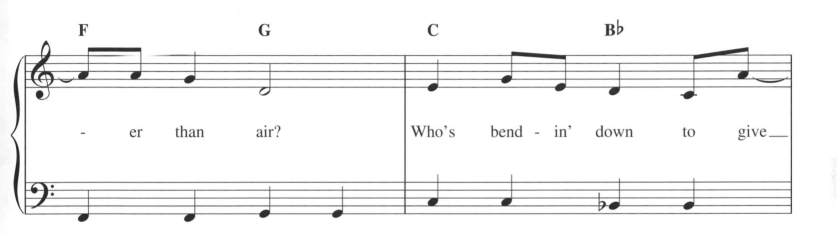

- er than air? Who's bend - in' down to give___

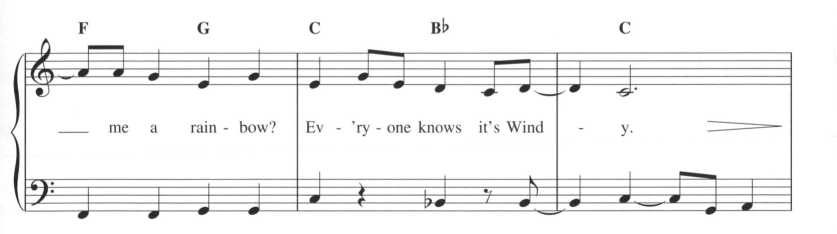

___ me a rain - bow? Ev - 'ry-one knows it's Wind - y.

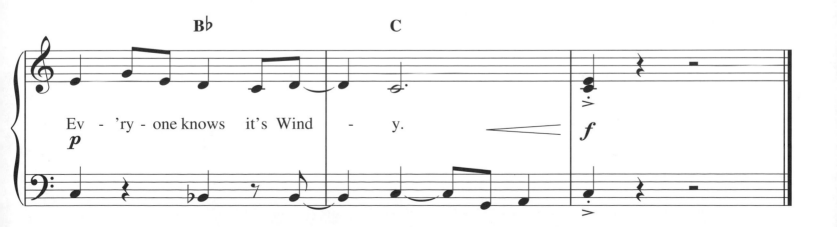

Ev - 'ry - one knows it's Wind - y.

*p*

*f*

# YOU'VE LOST THAT LOVIN' FEELIN'

Words and Music by BARRY MANN,
CYNTHIA WEIL and PHIL SPECTOR
Arranged by Phillip Keveren

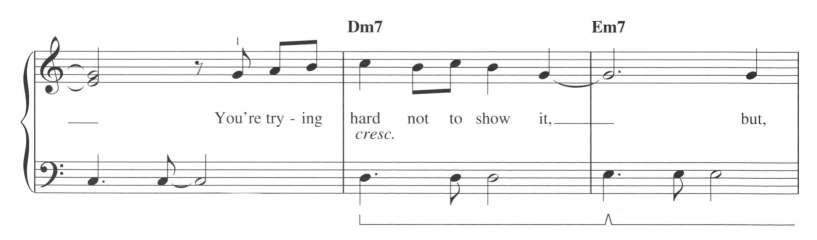

51

52

wel-come look___ in your eyes when I reach for you.___

Bb/C

___ And, girl, you're start-ing to___ crit-i-cize lit-tle things I

C

Dm7

do.___ It makes me just feel like cry-ing,___
*cresc.*

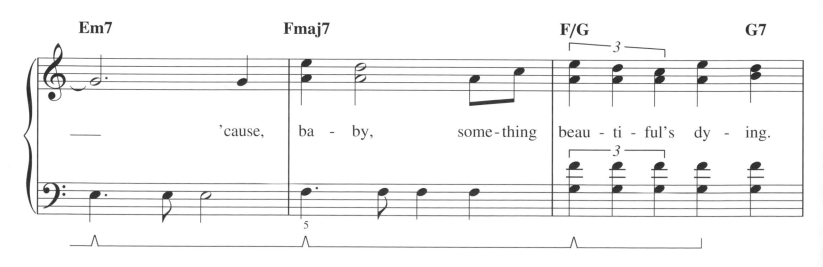

Em7                Fmaj7                           F/G            G7

___ 'cause, ba-by, some-thing beau-ti-ful's dy-ing.

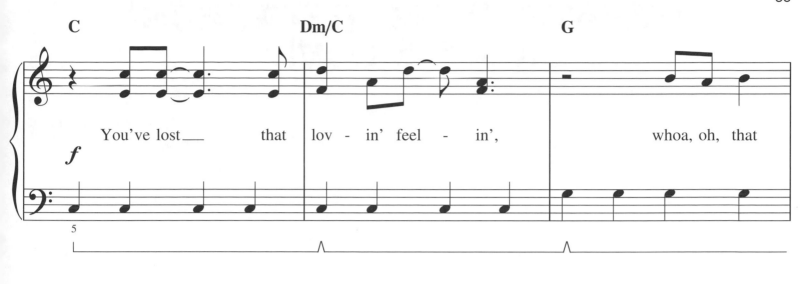

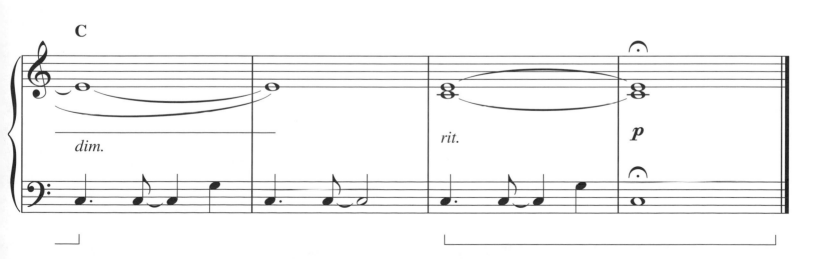

# WHAT THE WORLD NEEDS NOW IS LOVE

Lyric by HAL DAVID
Music by BURT BACHARACH
Arranged by Phillip Keveren

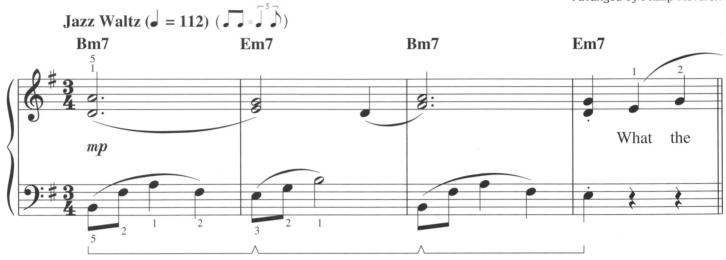

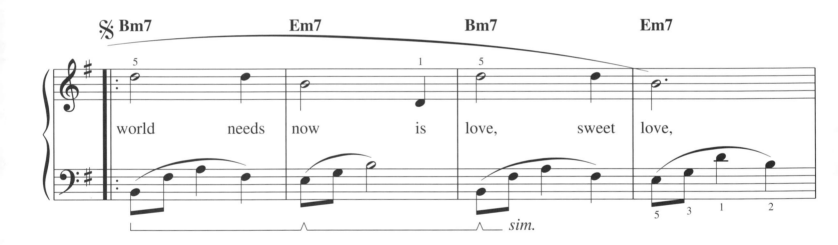